Contents

Acknowledgements

I must once again thank owners and breeders for their help in producing this book. Without their unflagging enthusiasm and willingness to answer a stream of questions, I would sit in front of a blank monitor. Thanks also to my grand-daughter Rebecca, whose pithy comments spur me on to readable texts. Finally, thank you to Professor D. Phillip Sponenberg of the Virginia-Maryland Regional College of Veterinary Medicine for his help at the eleventh hour.

If there are mistakes they are mine and mine alone.

Picture Credits

(1) Jim Perkins, *(2)* VEBBS e.V, *(3)* Debbie Kingsley, *(4)* IberGour.com, *(5)* Agriculture and Horticulture Development Board (AHDB), *(6)* PJ's Farm, *(7)* Forthill Farm, *(8)* Professor D Phillip Sponenberg, DVM, PHD, *(9)* 'Dever Hover' 58 jan@wtms.biz, *(10)* Cotswold Farm Park, *(11)* Penner Hampshires, Inc. John and Zella Penner, *(12)* Courtesy ACMC Ltd, (13) Cotswold Farm Park, *(14)* Hannah Smith, *(15)* www.oaklandpigs.co.uk, *(16)* Agriculture and Horticulture Development Board (AHDB), *(17)* Pig Paradise Farm, *(18)* Courtesy ACMC Ltd, *(19)* Courtesy ACMC Ltd, *(20)* www.oaklandpigs.co.uk, *(21)* Emile DeFelice, *(22)* Yorkshire Meats, Angus Turnbull, *(23)* H Jackman, Gillo Fawr Pedigree Pietrains, *(24)* Dr Esther Gallant, *(25)* Odds Farm Park, *(26)* Helen and Rob Rose, *(27)* The Welsh Pedigree Pig Society, Darren Davies, *(28)* Chris Grady, www.wildlifeimaging.co.uk, (New Breed) Simon and Sarah Righton, (RBST page) Hannah Smith.

Foreword

Pigs, hogs or swine, whatever you call them, have been around man for 11,000 years. Over these thousands of years they have provided us with food and, in earlier times, bones for tools and weapons, skin for shields and bristles for brushes.

Pigs are considered to have intelligence beyond that of a human three-year-old child. In the last few years, numbers of this bright-eyed animal have declined dramatically and a number of breeds have become extinct.

Whose fault is it? The government, the environment, the EU and food fashions must, to my mind, all take some of the blame. Rules and regulations created by people who know little about the industry and on occasions,

I feel, care even less. We should not discard breeds because they are currently unfashionable or do not fit in with the modern way of life.

The Rare Breeds Survival Trust does what it can to protect endangered species but we must all help preserve the rare and endangered animals on this fragile earth. As the tee-shirt slogan tells us, extinction is forever.

JACK BYARD
Bradford, 2009

1.

American Guinea Hog

Native to
America

Now found
In small numbers
in America

Description

Usually black but occasionally with a reddish tint. They have upright ears, a hairy coat and a curly tail.

The American Guinea Hog is a critically rare breed of pig that is unique to the USA. The original imported pigs came from the Canary Islands and West Africa in the 17th century.

The original Guinea Hog was crossed with several other breeds. Since these are now extinct it is impossible to create a complete and accurate picture of the true history of the breed. One possible cross is the small black Essex pig, also extinct, known to have lived in south-eastern USA where most Guinea hogs are to be found.

The American Guinea Hog was once expected to forage for its own food entirely and would eat roots, grass, nuts, rodents and even snakes. The breed is now kept on small farms and large ranches where they will keep the area clear of vermin. Their friendly, docile nature is an added bonus. This hardy little pig loves a good tummy rub and back scratch. It cannot be allowed to become extinct.

2.

Bentheim Black Pied

Native to
Lower Saxony in Germany

Now found
Throughout Europe

Description

The Bentheim Black Pied is white with black spots in grey rings and has lop ears.

The Bentheim Black Pied or Buntes Bentheimer Schwein originated at the beginning of the 20th century and was named after the district in Lower Saxony where it was first bred. It is a cross between local breeds of pig and the Berkshire. The Bentheim Black Pied was bred in the area until the late 1950s when tastes changed and demand for it declined. Extinction loomed.

The herd book was closed in 1964. One breeder kept meticulous records and the book was reopened in 1988 but numbers continued to decline. In 2003 the Association for the Conservation of the Bentheim Black Pied Pig came into being and things started to look brighter. The population of animals rose from 50 to 420 and registered breeders from 19 to 90 over four years.

When visiting Germany look for Benheim Black Pied products and help preserve this beautiful animal.

3.

Berkshire

Native to
The British Isles

Now found
In small groups
throughout the world

Protection category

Description

The Berkshire is black with prick ears, white socks, a white tip to the tail and a white flash on the face.

The Berkshire pig was discovered by Oliver Cromwell and his troops whilst in their winter quarters near Reading. It is reputed to be the oldest breed in Britain and is noted for its size and quality. The breed was improved in the 1700s with the introduction of Chinese and Siamese stock. For the past 200 years this bloodline has been kept pure. The original Berkshire was reddish or sandy-coloured and sometimes spotted. In the modern Berkshire, sandy-coloured hair is sometimes found in the white patches.

It is said that the Berkshire is at its best when given good housing and food. However in New Zealand, where it was established by early settlers, it wanders freely and is more inclined to graze.

When the Japanese Imperial family were presented with Berkshire hogs, the pork quickly became a delicacy. There are Japanese restaurants today that serve it exclusively. P G Wodehouse included a large Berkshire sow known as the Empress of Blandings in several of his books.

4.

Black Iberian/Spanish

Native to
Iberia

Now found
In the Mediterranean region

The Black Iberian is completely black or grey, including its hooves.

The Iberian pig is specific to the Mediterranean and is the last known breed to live entirely in the open; mainly under the cover of oak trees growing in Andalusia and the mountains of Spain. The micro-climate of the area is ideal for the oak tree's growth and consequently for the acorns which are the main food of the Black Iberian. It is this diet that helps to give the ham its unique flavour. The production is for quality not quantity.

The Iberian pig is rare but well regulated, only 15 pigs per hectare are allowed. The Iberian pig has a special place in the pig world; by sheer quality it has defied economics and the fickle public for centuries.

5.

British Landrace

Native to
Sweden

Now found
Throughout the world

Description

The British Landrace is white with a long muscular body and long drooping ears.

The Landrace breed of pig was imported to the British Isles from Sweden in 1949 to be studied in an independent evaluation carried out in York. Further imports were made into the British Isles for evaluation, to broaden the commercial base and allow further development into what was to become the British Landrace pig. Its broad genetic base makes this pig unique amongst landrace breeds throughout the world. The British Landrace is now found throughout the British Isles, mainly in Yorkshire and the Eastern Counties. It is also found in Scotland and Northern Ireland.

The Landrace Breed Society joined forces with the National Pig Breeders Association in 1978 and the British Isles is now one of the leading breeding countries of Landrace pigs which are exported worldwide. The British Landrace produces excellent pork and bacon.

6.

British Lop

Native to
The Tavistock area
of Cornwall

Now found
Throughout the British Isles
and France

Protection category

Description

A large white pig with lop ears.

The British Lop is one of the largest and most endangered native breeds. It is, apart from its colour, very similar to the Large Black. Originally the British Lop spread through the south-west of the British Isles to Dorset and Somerset but is now found throughout the country and also in France. In the Tavistock area it was known as the Devon Lop or the Cornish White. Prior to 1920 it went by the names: Long White; Lop-Eared Pig; or grandly, The National. Its present title was given in 1960. The British Lop is one of a group of Celtic breeds which included the Ulster, the Cumberland and the Lincolnshire Curly Coat which are now all extinct.

The British Lop is an excellent, docile mother and a hardy animal despite its pale skin. They are suited to outdoor breeding and with suitable shelter can remain outdoors all year round. Pigs, like humans, need protecting against sunburn but the British Lop needs little other specialist care and is suitable for small general farms. The breed produces pork and bacon of the highest quality.

7.

British Saddleback

Native to
East Anglia and the Isle of Purbeck on the Dorset and Hampshire borders

Now found
Throughout the British Isles, Nigeria and the Seychelles

Protection category

Description

Black apart from an unbroken white band over the shoulders and down to the front feet.

The Wessex Saddleback from the Isle of Purbeck, and the Essex from East Anglia were first recognised in herd books in 1918. The Essex was a finer, lighter pig with four white socks and a broad saddle; it was known as the Gent's pig. The Wessex had only two white socks at the front and was known as the Farmer's Choice.

The breeds were combined in 1967 and jointly called the British Saddleback. At this time numbers of the Essex were in sharp decline and some believe that, had the RBST been in existence in 1967, this amalgamation would not have occurred.

The British Saddleback is a hardy, docile animal and since its skin colour protects it from sunburn it is well suited to outdoor conditions. As for the flavour and succulence of Saddleback bacon, the experts have classed it as 'mouth-watering'.

8.

Choctaw Hog

Native to
America

Now found
Mainly in the Choctaw
Nation of Oklahoma

Description

The Choctaw is usually black but occasionally has white markings.

This pig is traditionally kept by the Choctaw Native Americans. The Choctaw Hog is a descendant of pigs which were brought to America in the 16th century by the Spaniards but were later bred by the Native Americans in the south-eastern states of the USA. When the Choctaw people moved from the Deep South to Oklahoma they took these pigs with them. Today's hogs are the direct descendants of the Oklahoma stock and their appearance has not changed in over 150 years.

The hogs are still reared in the traditional manner. They are earmarked and then released to run free, foraging for roots, acorns, berries and plants. They are periodically rounded up and sorted for market, breeding or meat and those that are released hurtle back into the woodland with surprising agility.

The Choctaw Hog is critically rare but does not have a high profile within the food industry so the money needed to preserve this part of American history has so far been slow in coming.

9.

Duroc

Native to
America

Now found
Throughout the British Isles
and on most continents

Description

The Duroc is golden brown to rich red mahogany.

In 1812 pigs known as Red Hogs were bred in New York and New Jersey. In 1823 Isaac Frink of Saratoga bought, from Harry Kelsey, a red boar whose parents were probably imported from Britain. Harry Kelsey owned a prize stallion called Duroc. The boar had his name. By the mid 19th century, systematic crossing of the red boar's descendants with the Red Hogs produced the modern Duroc.

In 1970 the Duroc was imported into the British Isles. It was not a roaring success. A second, more successful import was carried out in the 1980s, when the Meat and Livestock Commission carried out comprehensive trials to assess the merits of the breed. The Duroc has since found a place in British farming and a British version of the Duroc has been developed.

Their thick coat enables them to survive the British winters but the coat moults in summer allowing the Duroc to cope with the hot weather. Because of their colouring they are less prone to sunburn. The Duroc produces excellent pork and bacon.

10.

Gloucestershire Old Spots

Native to
The Vale of Berkeley on the banks of the river Severn

Now found
On most continents

Protection category

Description

Gloucestershire Old Spots have a white coat with clearly defined black spots and large floppy ears that cover their faces down to the snout.

The Gloucestershire Old Spots is the oldest pedigree spotted pig in the world.

It appears to be the result of crossing the original Gloucester with the unimproved Berkshire, a sandy-coloured pig with spots. The Gloucestershire Old Spots must have at least one spot. The fashion has changed over the years from very spotty pigs to ones where it was hard to find the single spot and back again.

The large docile Gloucestershire Old Spots is very hardy and, provided they have warm and dry shelter, they can happily spend the entire year outdoors. They once grazed orchards eating the windfall apples to supplement their diet. Indeed, Gloucestershire folklore has it that the spots are bruises from the falling fruit. Also known also as the Gloster Spot, Old Spot, The Cottager's Pig and The Orchard Pig.

11.

Hampshire

Native to
The British Isles

Now found
Throughout the world

Description

A black pig with a white belt. The belt is a strip of white across the shoulders and around the body covering the front legs. The ears are erect.

The Hampshire is thought to be the oldest early-American breed in existence. The original breeding pigs were Wessex or Wessex Saddleback crosses which were exported to America between 1825 and 1835 from a farm in Hampshire in the British Isles. The original American name was The Thin Rind but it was renamed the Hampshire in 1890.

The Hampshire as it is known today came from the Scottish borders. It was introduced into the British Isles in 1968 and thorough trials were carried out before it was released to British breeders. Further imports took place in 1970 from Canada since import restrictions created problems in importing from America. The Hampshire became very popular both here and worldwide. In the 1970s over 600 pigs were exported to 14 countries. In the world of pig breeding the Hampshire has found its place and produces quality pork and bacon.

Hybrid

Found
Worldwide

The hybrid sow is the type of sow used by commercial pig producers. It is created by breeding two distinct breeds or lines together and combines the best features of both the parent breeds.

Hybridisation has been carried out for thousands of years under many different names. In recent years the Large White x Landrace has traditionally been the most widely used hybrid sow in the UK. The pigs shown in the photograph opposite are first-cross hybrids of Meidam and Large White, known as hybrid AC1.

Some of the benefits of hybridisation are increased litter size, a greater resistance to disease, the ability to survive the vagaries of the weather and an improvement in the quality of the end product.

Iron Age

Found
On one or two farms
in Britain

Description

The Iron Age Pig is a dull brown colour.

The Iron Age pig is not a rare breed but reconstructed by a cross between a Tamworth sow and a Wild Boar to create a pig much like those that our Iron Age ancestors might have herded.

The Wild Boar lived in the British countryside before the Iron Age (750 BC-43 AD) and when crossed with a domesticated breed you should have pork as it used to taste and as many believe it should taste.

Iron Age pigs are more docile than Wild Boar but are not as easily handled as domestic breeds. The piglets have the same 'humbug' stripes as their Wild Boar ancestors.

The first Iron Age pigs were created at the Cotswold Farm Park in 1970 for a scientific reconstruction project. The idea was later copied by the BBC for their *Living in the Past* series. The Iron Age pig is bred mainly for the specialist meat trade.

14.

Kune Kune

Native to
New Zealand

Now found
In the British Isles,
Europe and the USA

The colour varies between ginger, brown, black, cream and spotted. They usually have a pair of tassels under the chin called Piri Piri.

Kune Kune (pronounced 'kooney kooney' - Maori for fat and round) pigs are from New Zealand but their true country of origin is in doubt. It is possible they were taken there by the Maoris since similar breeds can be found in Polynesia. Whalers from various countries released pigs on the islands to produce a food source for later visits. The pigs which came with Captain Cook on his first voyage to the island may also have contributed to the Kune Kune. The breed, also known as the Maori Pig, was brought to Britain in 1992 by Zoe Lindop and Andrew Calveley.

The Kune Kune is a delightful looking little pig with short legs and a short, round body. They are 60 to 67cm tall and can weigh from 63 kg to 109 kg. They are placid, easy to keep and enjoy human company. The Kune Kune feeds mainly on grass so are good lawn mowers, and they also produce excellent pork.

15.

Large Black

Native to
Devon, Cornwall
and East Anglia

Now found
In small herds
throughout the British
Isles and worldwide

Protection category

Description

They are always black.

The Large Black is Britain's only all-black pig. It originates from the Old English Hog in the 16th and 17th centuries. In the late 19th century there were two types of Large Black; one in Devon and Cornwall and another in East Anglia. These were brought together in 1889 by The Large Black Society.

The Large Black is found throughout the country and kept in small herds, some of which were established early in the 20th century. In the 1960s a trend toward intensive rearing led to a decline in the breed since it was unsuitable for this type of farming. Extremely docile and hardy, it is ideally suited to simple outdoor rearing systems. This characteristic and its colour made it popular for overseas breeding and by 1935 it had been exported to over 30 countries.

Large Black sows are excellent mothers able to bring up large litters off basic food. They once grazed orchards eating the windfall fruit and would be fed whey, a by-product of butter production. The Large Black produces superb quality meat.

16.

Large White

Native to
Yorkshire

Now found
Throughout the British Isles, the USA and Canada

Description

White hair, pink skin, erect ears and a slightly dished face.

The history of the Large White is difficult to trace. Its origins go back to Yorkshire in the north of England. It first came to prominence at the Royal Windsor Show in 1831 and was registered as a breed in 1884. It is believed the Large White was the result of a cross between the Cumberland, Leicestershire, Middle White and Small White breeds which were owned by John Tulley of Keighley, as well as Chinese and Siamese pigs. The Small White become extinct in 1912 and the last Cumberland died in Cumbria in 1960.

The Large White was bred to be almost self sufficient and is happy spending its life foraging outdoors. It is hardy and can withstand varying and extreme climates as well as producing large litters. By the end of the 19th century the Large White was well established worldwide and is said to be the world's favourite breed of pig.

In the USA and Canada it is known as the Yorkshire and produces excellent quality meat under any name.

Mangalitza

Native to
Hungary and Austria

Now found
Throughout the British Isles, the USA, Canada and Europe.

Description

The Mangalitza can be: Swallow Bellied – black with a white belly; Blonde – grey to yellow; or Red – a similar colour to the Tamworth.

The Mangalitza is an ancient pig with curly wool. In the early part of the 20th century it was crossed with the Lincolnshire Curly Coat which had been exported to Hungary and Austria. The Lincolnshire Curly Coat became extinct in 1972.

Mangalitza meat products were at one time in great demand all over Europe and were traded on the Vienna Stock Exchange. The breed was famed for its hardiness which was due, in part, to the woolly curly coat which gives superb insulation.

It is able to survive the harshest winters and long hot summers without the problems of sunburn.

In 2006, Tony York of Pig Paradise imported three males - one of each colour - and 14 females with hopes to establish herds of this excellent breed in the British Isles. Traditionally the meat is used for salami and Parma Ham because of its superb flavour.

Meidam

Native to
The British Isles

Now found
On most continents

Description

The Meidam is white with pink skin and semi-lop ears. Its conformation is similar to that of a Landrace but it is slightly shorter.

The Meidam (pronounced 'maydam') is a modern breed, accepted and registered at the beginning of the 21st century. Its genetic make-up is approximately a quarter Meishan, a quarter Large White and half Landrace. The aim is to capture the advantages of the Meishan sow which are larger litter sizes and excellent mothering ability. At the same time, the new breed retains the European breeds' benefits of growth rate and excellent lean meat.

So this is a 'synthetic' breed, created with a commercial purpose, but using the genes of long-established pure breeds.

This is not the first time Chinese pig genes have been used to establish a 'native' British breed. It is thought that in the 1800s an importation of Chinese pigs was interbred with pigs that eventually contributed to the Large White breed.

19.

Meishan

Native to
China

Now found
On most continents

Description

The Meishan is black with a heavily wrinkled face and skin. Their flop ears cover their eyes.

The Meishan (pronounced 'mayshawn') comes from a narrow belt of land between north and central China in the lower Changjiang river basin. It is an area of lakes and valleys with a mild climate. The pigs are well-fed on farm by-products, water plants and concentrates. The Meishan is fat and slow-growing but has excellent flavoured meat.

The breed was first imported into the British Isles in the 1980s. Upon seeing two Meishan lying down, one man remarked 'it's like looking at a pile of old coats'. The Meishan is relatively disease resistant, docile and an extremely good mother. It is usually crossed with the Large White to produce excellent quality meat. The best of Yorkshire and China brought together for a superb result.

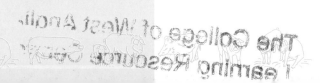

Middle White

Native to
Keighley in West Yorkshire

Now found
Throughout the British Isles
and worldwide

Protection category

Description

A thick white coat, snub nose, dished face and large pricked ears.

The Middle White was first recognised in 1852 at an agricultural show in West Yorkshire. At the show they were exhibited, by Mr Joseph Tulley, alongside the Large White and the Small White. The judges agreed about the fine quality of the breed but felt they were too small for Large Whites and too large for Small Whites and so a third class for the Middle White was born. It is now the smallest British pig; the Small White became extinct in 1912.

The breed was created by crossing local breeds with Chinese and Siamese pigs from which the Middle White inherits its characteristic dished face. The placid Middle White, often described as the 'beautifully ugly' pig, is exported worldwide and is in great demand in Japan where it is known as the Middle Yorks.

In 1990 the Middle White Pig Breeders Club was created with the chef Antony Worral Thompson as patron. The succulent meat of the Middle White is much darker than that of other breeds.

21.

Ossabaw Island Hog

Native to
Ossabaw Island off the coast of Georgia in America

Now found
On Ossabaw Island and a few in Georgia

Description

These hogs are black, spotted black-and-white or red-and-tan. They have heavy coats, pricked-up ears and long snouts.

The pigs of Ossabaw Island are an extremely rare breed native to the southern states of America. They are descendants of the animals brought to this New World island by the Spaniards over 450 years ago. In most environments feral pigs will cross with domestic breeds but this is not the case on Ossabaw Island. They have developed and bred in total isolation.

In spring, food is in short supply so over the centuries the Ossabaw Island Hog has adapted to the food cycle with a method of storing fat to see them over the periods when food is scarce. Over time they have also become smaller.

Because of quarantine restrictions it is not possible to import the pigs directly from the island. The herds on the mainland today are descended from a group that left the island in 1970, prior to the restrictions. The meat is of superb quality with a fat profile high in Omega 3s and beautifully marbled with a rich wild flavour.

22.

Oxford Sandy and Black

Native to
Oxfordshire

Now found
Throughout the British Isles

Description

They are pale to dark gold with black blotches - not spots. The ears are lopped or semi-lopped. The boar has a white tip to the tail, four white feet and, for perfection, a white blaze.

The Oxford Sandy and Black has been in existence for over 300 years and was a traditional cottager's pig around Oxfordshire. It is one of the oldest pig breeds in the British Isles. In the 1940s the breed was on the decline and by 1985 extinction appeared inevitable. Were it not for the efforts of three dedicated men, the Oxford Sandy and Black would be no more.

The main body colour is due to its Tamworth ancestry. The Oxford Sandy and Black is also known as the Plum Porridge, the Plum Pudding and the Oxford Forest. The Oxford Sandy and Black is happiest outdoors foraging in woodland and rough grazing. Its colour gives it greater protection against sunburn and its long coat makes it tolerant of wet weather.

The Oxford Sandy and Black is a amiable animal to manage so is ideal for smallholders and produces meat of excellent quality and flavour.

23.

Pietrain

Native to
Belgium

Now found
Mainly in Belgium
and the UK

Description

A medium-sized pig with a white coat and black spots which have a lighter surround. The ears are erect.

The Pietrain originates in 1940 and takes its name from the town in Belgium where it was bred. It is a cross between a local large white Landrace-type pig and the French Bayeux, which itself is descended from the Berkshire. The breeding was small scale until after the 2nd World War when the Pietrain began to be noticed for its quality meat.

In the 1960s an attempt was made to import 64 animals aiming to improve quality and reduce cost. None survived the journey. Another attempt was made in the 1970s but this was not a success. The knowledgeable put this down to poor animal husbandry, others to Porcine Stress Syndrome although this seldom occurs in animals that have been well bred and handled. The Royal Welsh Festival has pig agility races through cones and hoops just for fun. It is frequently won by a healthy, happy Pietrain. Their low fat meat regularly wins National gold and silver medals for its quality.

24.

Poland China

Native to
The Miami Valley, Butler and Warren Counties, Ohio

Now found
In America and Cyprus

Description

The Poland China is a large black pig with white patches.

The breed owes its origins to so many different breeds of pig it is difficult to know where to start. In 1816 John Wallace bought four Big China Hogs, one boar and three sows. Two of the sows were white and the third had black spots. These Big China Hogs were popular in Virginia, Maryland, Pennsylvania and Kentucky. There is also evidence pointing to the bloodline of pigs bred by the Duke of Bedford which have similar colouring and came from Kentucky about this time. Whatever their origins, the quality of meat is superb.

There were two important requirements when breeding a Poland China: it had to be large and it had to be able to travel; pigs were driven to market and this frequently meant a journey of a hundred miles.

If you are in USA or Cyprus, look out for the Poland China – they are magnificent animals.

25.

Tamworth

Native to
Staffordshire

Now found
In the British Isles, New Zealand, the USA, Australia and Canada.

Protection category

Description

Tamworths are a rich golden brown.

Tamworth pigs originated in Staffordshire in the early 19th century and it is possibly the purest of English native pigs. It is classed as being rather primitive because of its long snout - the longest of any modern breed - and pricked-up ears. Credit for its colour is due to the introduction of a red boar from Ireland.

The Tamworth became well established and, thanks to its adaptability, by the end of the 19th century it was being exported to Australia, North America and South East Asia. Records from the early 20th century show pigs similar to the Tamworth running wild in the Otago region of South Island, New Zealand.

The Tamworth is ideal for rearing in outdoor systems and is used for reclaiming wood and scrubland. It is the perfect four-legged ploughing machine. In winter they will quite happily live in a hut in a snow-covered field. Their golden brown colour gives protection from sunburn which is a serious problem for the paler coloured breeds. Although rare, the Tamworth is still bred for meat.

26.

Vietnamese Pot Bellied

Native to
The Red River Delta in Vietnam

Now found
In the British Isles, America, Canada, Europe, the Middle East, Indonesia, Japan and Vietnam.

Description

Vietnamese Pot Bellies are black with wrinkled skin, especially around the face. They have small upright ears, a hanging belly, short legs and a short straight tail.

There are approximately 2.5 million Vietnamese Pot Bellied pigs in Vietnam. They arrived in Europe and the USA in the 1960s and were popular with zoos and animal parks during the 1970s. In the 1980s the idea of keeping a pig as a pet took off. In America in 1986 a pig cost several thousand dollars.

The original Vietnamese Pot Bellies were not ideal house pets but since then the breed has been improved beyond belief and is now a good pet for those with a large garden or a smallholding as they have an extremely good temperament. A modern fully-grown animal can weigh from 30 kg to 100 kg and the male is the smaller of the two. As the Vietnamese Pot Bellied has been crossed with many other breeds it is considered impossible to find a pure-bred.

Welsh

Native to
Wales and the British Isles

Now found
Wales and the British Isles

Protection category

Description

The Welsh pig is white with lop ears meeting just short of the snout. The perfect Welsh pig is pear-shaped when viewed from above or either side.

Originally the Welsh pig came to prominence in 1870 when large numbers were sold into Cheshire for fattening on milk by-products. The Welsh Pig Society was founded in 1920. The Old Glamorgan Pig Society represented breeds similar to the Welsh from the Cardigan, Pembroke and Carmarthen areas. The two societies amalgamated in 1922 to become the Welsh Pig Society.

The Welsh reached its peak in popularity in 1947. In 1955 the scientist Dr. J. Hammond advised the government that the Welsh pig was one of the three breeds on which the British pig industry should be founded (the other two being the Large White and the Landrace). The Welsh is a hardy breed and will thrive under most conditions, indoors or out. The breed is now at risk with less than 200 in Wales and less than 600 in the British Isles.

28.

Wild Boar

Four main groups of boar
covered the world

Now found
At large in the UK in
East Kent, Sussex, Devon,
Fort William and Dumfries
and Galloway

Description

The thick bristly coat is brown, reddish brown, black or dark grey and the bristles are tipped with white or tan. A ridge of bristles runs down the spine. They have a soft hair undercoat called a pelage. The male has upper and lower tusks; the female has smaller lower tusks only.

The Wild Boar is the ancestor of the modern-day domestic pig. It became extinct in the British Isles for the first time in the early 14th century but was reintroduced by James I and his son who brought them from Germany to the New Forest. They were not popular with the local residents and created devastation wherever they appeared. Before the end of the 17th century the British Isles was once more a Wild Boar free zone.

It was almost 300 years before they re-appeared on British farms. Released from captivity either through accident or design, there are several 'sounders' (a group of feral Wild Boar) now roaming the British countryside. The young borelets have brown and white stripes which are excellent camouflage when hiding in the undergrowth. The meat is red to rose coloured and apparently tastes like 'best beef with crackling'.

Glamrock

Black, white, ginger with spots and speckles.

As a result of feedback from their customers, pig breeders Simon and Sarah Righton decided to produce a breed that retained the intense flavour of their Gloucestershire Old Spots whilst being more acceptable for the modern health-conscious market.

The boar chosen for this task was a Hamroc, itself a cross between the Duroc and the Hampshire. The colour variations of the piglets were no great surprise; no litter has two identical piglets and combines the spots of the Gloucestershire Old Spots sow, the black and white of the Hampshire and the ginger of the Duroc.

RBST
Rare Breeds Survival Trust

The Watchlist covers endangered breeds of cattle, goats, horses, pigs, poultry and sheep native to the British Isles.

A breed whose numbers of registered breeding females are estimated by the Rare Breeds Survival Trust to be below the Category 6 'Mainstream' threshold will be accepted into the appropriate Watchlist category.

In this book I have highlighted the first five categories.

 Critical

Endangered

Vulnerable

At Risk

Minority

The Rare Breeds Survival Trust only covers British native breeds and so these categories are not relevant to all the breeds in this book.

Further information: www.rbst.org.uk

Pig Talk

Sow	–	*A female pig*
Boar	–	*A male pig*
Piglet	–	*A baby pig of eight weeks old or less*
Gilt	–	*A young sow*
Litter	–	*The brood of young born to a pig*
Shoat	–	*A young pig which has just been weaned*
Farrow	–	*A litter of piglets*
Hog/Swine	–	*Other terms for pig*